A NOTE TO PARENTS AND TEACHERS

Smithsonian Readers were created for children who are just starting on the amazing road to reading. These engaging books support the acquisition of reading skills, encourage children to learn about the world around them, and help to foster a lifelong love of books. These high-interest informational texts contain fascinating, real-world content designed to appeal to beginning readers. This early access to high-quality books provides an essential reading foundation that students will rely on throughout their school career.

The four levels in the Smithsonian Readers series target different stages of learning abilities. Each child is unique; age or grade level does not determine a particular reading level. See the inside back cover for complete descriptions of each reading level.

When sharing a book with beginning readers, read in short stretches, pausing often to talk about the pictures. Have younger children turn the pages and point to the pictures and familiar words. And be sure to reread favorite parts. As children become more independent readers, encourage them to share the ideas they are reading about and to discuss ideas and questions they have. Learning practice can be further extended with the quizzes after each title and the included fact cards.

There is no right or wrong way to share books with children. You are setting a pattern of enjoying and exploring books that will set a literacy foundation for their entire school career. Find time to read with your child, and pass on the amazing world of literacy.

Adria F. Klein, Ph.D.
Professor Emeritus
California State University San Bernardino

Smithsonian

READERS

Early Adventures

LEVEL 1

Safari Animals

Animal Habitats

Insects

Vehicles

Outer Space

Reptiles

Silver Dolphin Books
An imprint of Printers Row Publishing Group
10350 Barnes Canyon Road, Suite 100, San Diego CA 92121
www.silverdolphinbooks.com

ISBN 978-1-62686-451-1
Manufactured, printed, and assembled in Dongguan City, China
19 18 17 16 15 1 2 3 4 5

Animal Habitats and Vehicles written by Kaitlyn DiPerna
Outer Space and Insects written by Ruth Strother
Reptiles written by Brenda Scott Royce
Safari Animals written by Emily Rose Oachs
Edited by Kaitlyn DiPerna
Editorial Assistance by Courtney Acampora
Cover Design by Jenna Riggs
Cover Production by Rusty von Dyl
Book Design by Kat Godard
Animal Habitats, Reptiles, Safari Animals, and Insects reviewed by Dr. Don E. Wilson,
        Curator Emeritus of the Department of Vertebrate Zoology, National Museum of
        Natural History, Smithsonian
Outer Space reviewed by Andrew K. Johnston, Geographer for the Center for Earth and
        Planetary Studies, National Air and Space Museum, Smithsonian
Vehicles reviewed by F. Robert van der Linden, chairman of the Aeronautics Division,
        National Air and Space Museum, Smithsonian

For Smithsonian Enterprises:
Kealy Gordon, Product Development Manager, Licensing
Ellen Nanney, Licensing Manager
Brigid Ferraro, Vice President, Education and Consumer Products
Carol LeBlanc, Senior Vice President, Education and Consumer Products
Chris Liedel, President

HOW TO USE THIS BOOK

Glossary

As you read each title, you will see words in **bold letters**. More information about these words can be found in the glossary at the end of each title.

Quizzes

Multiple-choice quizzes are included at the end of each title. Use these quizzes to check your understanding of the topic. Answers are printed at the end of the quiz, or you can reread the title to check your answers.

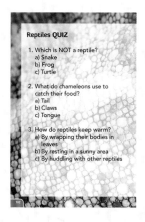

Fact Cards

Each title comes with six tear-out fact cards. Read the cards for fun or use them as quizzes with a friend or family member. You'll be impressed with all you can learn!

ABOUT THE SMITHSONIAN

Founded in 1846, the Smithsonian is the world's largest museum and research complex, consisting of 19 museums and galleries, the National Zoological Park, and nine research facilities. The Smithsonian's vision is to shape the future by preserving our heritage, discovering new knowledge, and sharing our resources with the world.

Brightly colored parrots fly through the rain forest.

Monkeys swing on jungle branches.

Jungle leopards' spots help them hide in the shadows.

Wide Open Savannas

Savannas are wide-open spaces with tall grasses.

Savannas are hot and dry.

Savannas do not get much rain.

When it does rain, grass grows and animals have water to drink.

Lions hunt in the tall grasses.

Elephants play in the water.
Giraffes eat leaves from tall trees.

Zebras gather in **herds**. Their stripes
help them to blend together.

Extreme Deserts

Deserts are very dry places.
Some deserts do not have any rain for years!

Deserts can be very hot during the day.
Deserts can be very cold at night.

Camels can survive without water for days.

Owls hunt at night, when it is cooler.

Rattlesnakes hide in the shade of rocks and plants.

At night, coyotes call to each other across the desert: "Owoooah!"

Earth's Forests

Forests have cold winters and warm summers.

Some forest animals survive by **hibernating** in the winter.

They go into a deep sleep for months!

Foxes use their bushy tails as a warm cover in the cold.

Grizzly bears stand in streams to catch their favorite meal: salmon.

Porcupines have sharp quills for protection.

Male deer grow antlers in the summer.

The antlers fall off in the winter!

Mountain Life

Mountains have high winds, ice, and snow. Mountains are rocky and rugged.

Animals that live in the mountains have to be good climbers.

Mountain goats have hooves that can grip the rocky ground.

Groups of llamas live together in herds on mountainsides.

Chinchillas have soft, thick fur to keep them warm.

Mountain lions are **predators**. They hunt other animals for food.

The Icy Polar Regions

The South and North Poles are extremely cold.

Ice covers the poles year-round.

Arctic animals have special features to protect them against the cold.

Penguins' feathers are waterproof to keep them dry when they swim to find fish. When the penguins are on land, they huddle together in groups to keep warm.

Polar bears' cream-colored coats help to hide them against the snowy landscape.

Walruses and leopard seals come onto the ice to rest.

Unique Islands

An island is a small piece of land surrounded by water.

Islands can be home to **unique** animals that can't be found anywhere else.

More than one hundred different types of lemurs live on the island of Madagascar.

Kiwi birds are native to New Zealand.

These small birds cannot fly.

Flying foxes aren't foxes at all. They are bats that eat fruit!

Galapagos giant tortoises live to be over one hundred years old!

Komodo dragons are huge lizards that can grow to be ten feet long!

They eat nearly anything, including pigs, goats, and even other Komodo dragons.

Freshwater: Lakes, Rivers, and Ponds

Only three percent of the water on Earth is fresh water.

Fresh water can be found in tiny puddles or great lakes, in small streams and mighty rivers.

Many fish that live in rivers have to be strong swimmers so they don't get pulled by the **current**.

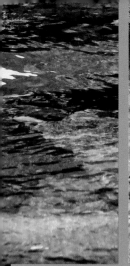

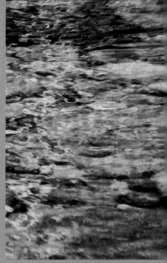

Salmon live in the ocean but they swim up rivers to where they were born.

Canada geese **migrate** when winter is coming.

They fly long distances to warmer weather.

Beavers use their strong teeth to cut down small trees and branches.

They use the branches to build dams.

Wetlands and Swamps

Wetlands and swamps are areas with shallow water and grasses.

Wetlands and swamps may be freshwater or saltwater, like the ocean.

The Everglades is a flooded wetland and a national park.

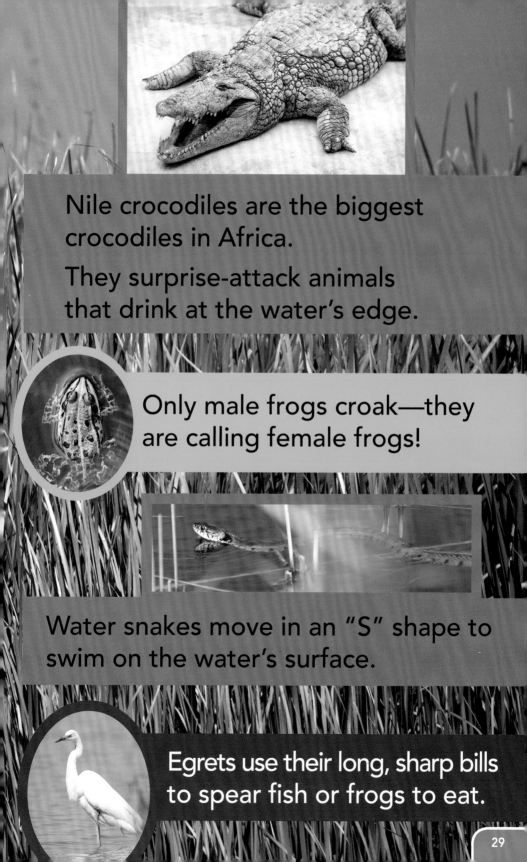

Nile crocodiles are the biggest crocodiles in Africa.

They surprise-attack animals that drink at the water's edge.

Only male frogs croak—they are calling female frogs!

Water snakes move in an "S" shape to swim on the water's surface.

Egrets use their long, sharp bills to spear fish or frogs to eat.

Coastal Waters and Tide Pools

Coastal waters are the shallow parts of the ocean by the shore.

Tide pools are rocky pools by the shore that fill with water.

The tide affects coastal waters and tide pools.

The tide causes the ocean to rise and fall twice each day.

Manatees and dugongs are gentle giants that live in warm coastal waters.
They are mammals, so they need to come to the water's surface to breathe.

Sea otters float on their backs.
They hold onto kelp so they don't float away.

Most sea stars have five arms, but some have ten, twenty, or even forty arms!

Colorful Coral Reefs

Coral reefs are made from tiny animals called polyps.

The polyps have a hard shell like a snail.

The polyps join together and their shells make a reef.

Coral reefs are home to more types of fish than anywhere else in the ocean.

Reef sharks have sharp, triangular teeth.

Sea turtles feed at coral reefs.

Sea turtles only go on land to lay eggs.

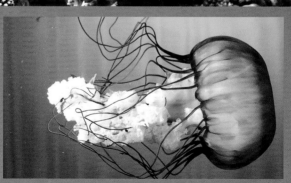

Jellyfish are not fish, but they do feel like jelly!

But don't try to touch them—some sting!

The Open Ocean

The ocean covers more than seventy percent of Earth's surface.

The open ocean has warm tropical waters, and cold icy waters.

Many ocean animals migrate long distances in the ocean to find food.

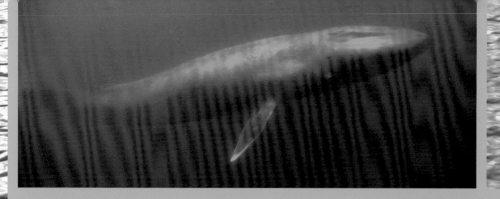

Blue whales are the largest animals on the planet.

The heart of a blue whale can weigh as much as a car!

Dolphins travel in groups called pods.

They talk to each other with whistles and squeaks.

Flying fish can swim fast enough to break the water's surface and glide through the air!

Protecting Animal Habitats

Animals are only able to live in certain habitats.

Some habitats are disappearing.

Forests are being cut down.

Polar ice is melting.

It is important to protect animal habitats. We can protect habitats by recycling, using cars less, and not **polluting**.

We want all the animals on Earth to have a home!

Animal Habitats QUIZ

1. Which habitat does a lion live in?

    a) Savanna

    b) Desert

    c) Rain forest

2. Which habitat is home to more than half of the animals on Earth?

    a) Rain forest

    b) Freshwater

    c) Desert

3. What does hibernating mean?

    a) Hunting for food

    b) Finding a mate

    c) Going into a deep sleep

4. Where are kiwi birds from?

    a) Africa

    b) New Zealand

    c) Madagascar

5. What are coral reefs made from?

    a) Algae

    b) Polyps

    c) Krill

6. The ocean covers how much of Earth's surface?

    a) Seven percent

    b) Seventy percent

    c) Fifty percent

Answers: 1) a 2) a 3) c 4) b 5) b 6) b

GLOSSARY

current: water moving in a certain direction

habitat: place where an animal lives

herds: large groups of hoofed animals

hibernating: going into a deep sleep during the winter

migrate: to move from one area to another for feeding or breeding

 **polluting:** spoiling something with trash and waste

predators: animals that hunt and eat other animals for food

unique: unlike anything else

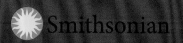

Outer Space

Ruth Strother

Contents

Endless Space

Outer space is huge.
The universe contains everything
we can see.
No one knows where it ends.
Stars, planets, and moons can be
found in outer space.

Stars

Stars are bright balls of burning gas.
Stars can burn for billions of years.
The Sun is a star.
It is the closest star to Earth.

People draw pretend lines between some stars.
The lines form shapes.
The shapes look like people and animals.
These shapes are called **constellations**.

The Solar System

The Sun is the only star in our solar system.
The Sun is the center of our solar system.
The word *solar* means "of the Sun."

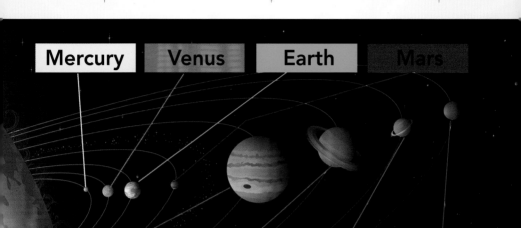

Mercury Venus Earth Mars

Jupiter Saturn Uranus Neptune

The Sun's **gravity** pulls planets into a path. The path leads planets around the Sun.

We live on the planet Earth.
Earth is part of the solar system.

Planets

Planets are objects in space.
Planets must follow a path around a star.
Our solar system has eight planets.

Each planet is round.
Each planet follows a path around the Sun.
This path is called an **orbit**.
And each planet is the only big object in its orbit.

Four planets are closer to the Sun.
They are Mercury, Venus, Earth, and Mars.
They are the inner planets.

Inner planets are small, solid, and rocky.

Mercury is the smallest planet in the solar system.

Venus is the brightest planet seen from Earth.

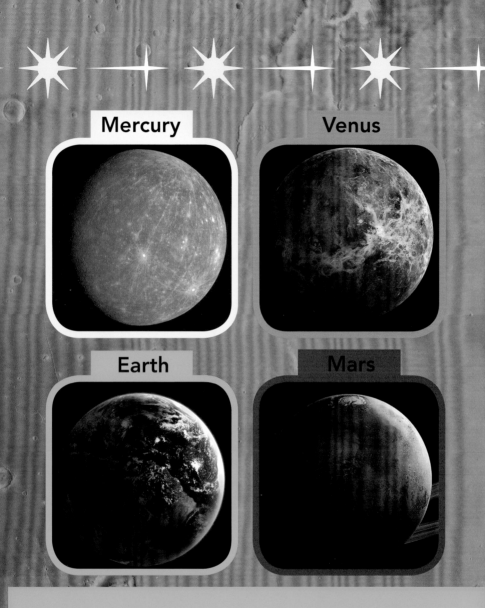

Mercury

Venus

Earth

Mars

Earth is the only planet with liquid water on its surface.

Mars has the tallest mountain in the solar system.

Gas Planets

Saturn

Neptune

Jupiter

Uranus

The gas planets are Jupiter, Saturn, Uranus, and Neptune. They are not solid. They are gassy, almost like clouds. Spaceships can't land on them.

Jupiter is the biggest planet in the solar system.

Saturn has rings made of ice, dust, and rocks.

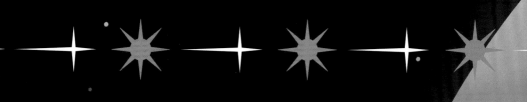

Uranus is the coldest planet in the solar system.

Neptune is the windiest planet in the solar system.

Jupiter

Saturn

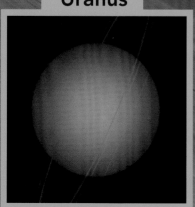

Uranus

Neptune

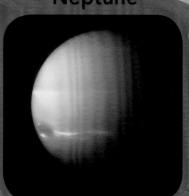

Moons

Moons are space objects.
Moons orbit a planet.
The planet's gravity keeps a moon on its path.

Some planets have many moons.
Some planets have no moon at all.

Earth has one moon.

Jupiter has more moons than any other planet.
Jupiter has sixty-seven moons!

Comets are dust and rocks trapped in ice.
Comets orbit the Sun.
Comets have a tail.
The tail points away from the Sun.

Comets melt a little when they get close to the Sun.
Some comets crash into a planet or a moon.
These comets leave big holes called **craters**.

Asteroids and Meteoroids

Asteroids are made of rocks.
Asteroids orbit the Sun, just like planets do.
But asteroids are too small to be planets.
Most asteroids are found between Mars and Jupiter.

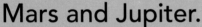

Meteoroids are made of rocks and metals.
Meteoroids are smaller than asteroids.
But meteoroids orbit the Sun too.
Sometimes asteroids and meteoroids fall to Earth.

Meteors, Meteorites, and Shooting Stars

Meteors are meteoroids that get close to Earth.
Meteors burn when they get close to Earth.
Meteors look like flashes of light.
We call them shooting stars!

Sometimes meteors don't burn up.
Sometimes meteors land on Earth.
Then they are called meteorites.

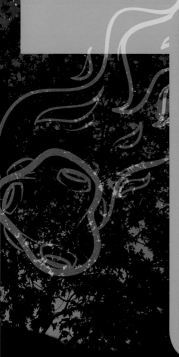

Galaxies

Galaxies are made of dust, gas, and billions of stars.
Billions of galaxies spin in outer space.
Earth and our solar system are part of a galaxy.

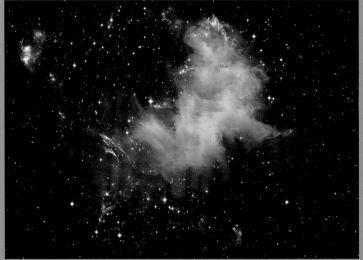

Our galaxy has hundreds of billions of stars!
From Earth, the stars look like a pathway of milk.
Our galaxy is called the Milky Way.

Astronauts

Astronauts travel to outer space. Some astronauts learn how to fly a spaceship.

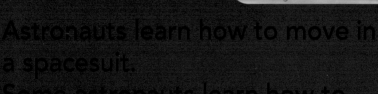

Astronauts learn how to move in a spacesuit.
Some astronauts learn how to study outer space.

astronauts

American astronauts train at NASA.
But astronauts come from other
countries too.

Astronauts are called cosmonauts
in Russia.
The first person in space
was a cosmonaut.

cosmonaut

Spaceships and Space Stations

The first spaceship was the size of a soccer ball.

Now spaceships are big. Spaceships carry astronauts into outer space.

Some astronauts live and work in space.

Their job is to study outer space. They stay in outer space for many months. These astronauts live and work in space stations.

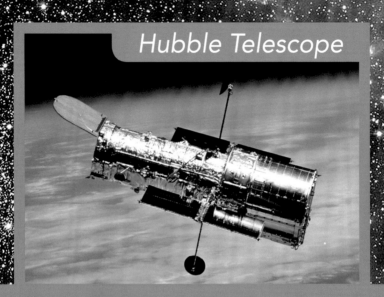

Hubble Telescope

We can't get to many parts of outer space.
So we send up robots and **telescopes**.
They explore space for us.
They send us new facts.

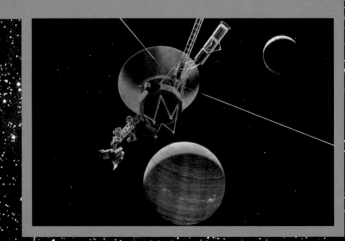

Mars Rover

We have a lot of outer space to explore.
Maybe someday you will be an astronaut.
Maybe you will work in a space station.
Maybe you will explore a new planet!

Outer Space QUIZ

1. How long can stars burn?
   a) Thousands of years
   b) Hundreds of years
   c) Billions of years

2. What does the word "solar" mean?
   a) "of outer space"
   b) "of the Sun"
   c) "of a star"

3. How many planets are in our solar system?
   a) Eight
   b) Five
   c) Nine

4. Which is the smallest planet in our solar system?
   a) Earth
   b) Jupiter
   c) Mercury

5. Which is the biggest planet in our solar system?
   a) Jupiter
   b) Saturn
   c) Mars

6. What is our galaxy called?
   a) A constellation
   b) The solar system
   c) The Milky Way

GLOSSARY

 **constellations**: groups of stars that form shapes

craters: scooped-out areas made by space objects hitting a planet or moon

gravity: a force that pulls one object to another

 **orbit**: the path one object takes around another object

telescope: a tool that makes distant objects look closer and bigger

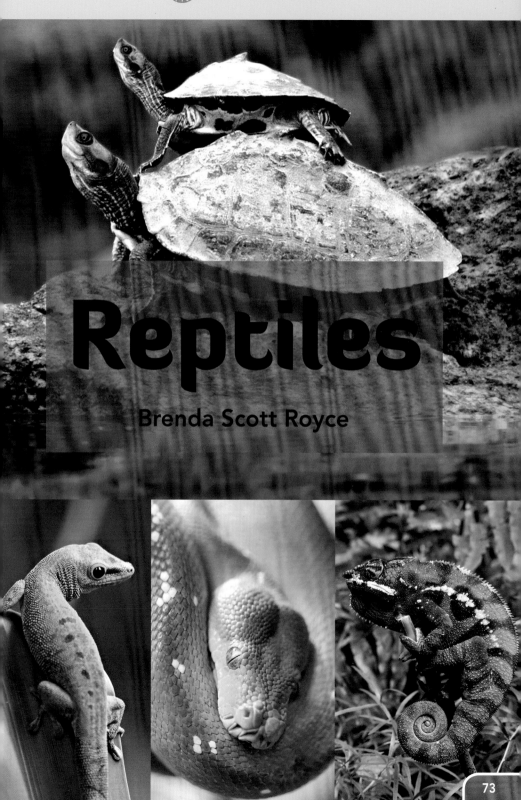

Reptiles

Brenda Scott Royce

Contents

What Is a Reptile?

Snakes, turtles, lizards, and alligators are all types of reptiles.
There are more than eight thousand types of reptiles in the world!

Really Cool Reptiles

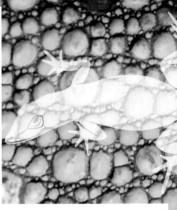

The Galapagos tortoise is the world's largest tortoise.
This giant tortoise weighs more than a full-grown gorilla!

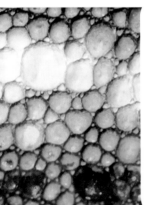

The male Jackson's chameleon has three horns on his head.

The blue-tongued skink is named for the color of its tongue.

Lizards cannot fly.
But the Draco lizard comes close.
The Draco lizard has flaps of skin on both sides of its body.
It spreads these flaps and glides in the wind!

Reptile Homes

Reptiles live all over the world, except in Antarctica.
A reptile's home is called its **habitat**. Different reptiles live in different types of habitats.

Some reptiles live in the desert.

Others hang out in the jungle.

Reptiles can be found in lakes, rivers, and oceans.

What's for Dinner?

Different reptiles eat different foods.
Small reptiles eat insects.
A chameleon catches a cricket with
its long, sticky tongue.

Desert tortoises eat grass, plants,
and flowers.

Snakes are meat eaters.
They eat other animals.
Snakes' favorite foods are mice,
birds, eggs, and frogs.

Shells and Scales

Reptiles may be smooth, rough, or bumpy.
Reptiles are not slimy!

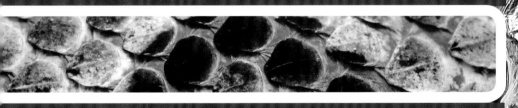

Snake skin is made up of **scales**.
Snake scales come in different shapes and colors.
Scales overlap like tiles on the roof of a house.

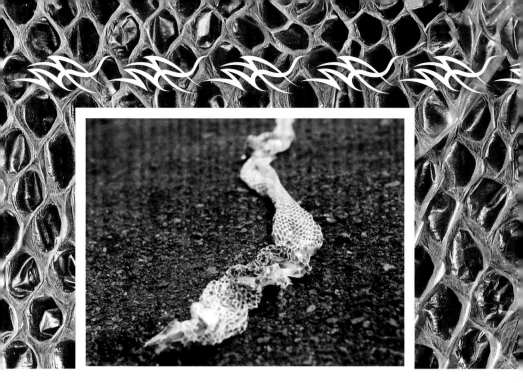

Reptiles replace their skin as they grow. A snake sheds its skin all at once.

Turtles and tortoises have hard shells. The star tortoise has star-shaped markings on its shell.

Reptiles don't have fur or feathers. So how do they stay warm? Reptiles are cold-blooded. Cold-blooded means they cannot control their body heat.

Reptiles need heat from the sun to keep warm.
A lizard rests on a rock in a sunny area.
When it gets too hot, the lizard will move to a shady spot.

Hide and Seek

Some reptiles are great at hiding.
Their colors and patterns blend in
with rocks, branches, or trees.
A leaf gecko looks like a leaf.

Chameleons change color to
match their surroundings.

The Gaboon **viper** is a large snake that lives in the forest.
The patterns on the viper's back help it blend in with leaves on the forest floor.

The coral snake has pretty colors. But watch out! This snake has a dangerous bite.
The coral snake's bright colors warn others to stay away.

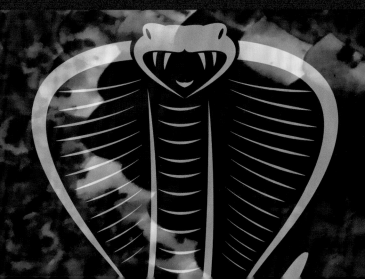

A rattle is this snake's alarm.
A rattlesnake wriggles the rattle at the end of its tail.
The sound tells others: "Beware!"

A cobra can spread out his neck to make himself appear bigger.
This is how the cobra frightens enemies.

Turtles and Tortoises

What's the difference between a turtle and a tortoise?

turtle

A tortoise is a type of turtle. Turtles are usually found near water.

tortoise

Tortoises live on land.

Turtles and tortoises have hard shells.
Shells protect turtles.
A turtle tucks its head and legs into
its shell for safety.

Turtles don't have teeth!
They bite their food with a sharp
upper beak.

Snakes eat other animals for food.
Some snakes kill their **prey** by squeezing it.
Boas and pythons are squeezers.

Other snakes kill their prey by biting it.
Rattlesnakes are biters.
Rattlesnakes have sharp teeth called **fangs**.
A rattlesnake uses its fangs to inject **venom** or poison into its prey.

Lizards

There are more than four thousand types of lizards.
Iguanas, chameleons, and geckos are all lizards.
A green iguana can be six feet long!

The gecko's toes are great at gripping! The gecko's special toes help it climb up walls.

This colorful creature is a collared lizard. The black stripes around its neck look like a shirt collar.

Dragons!

These are not fairytale dragons.
They cannot fly.
They don't breathe fire.
These dragons belong to the lizard family.
The Komodo dragon is the world's largest lizard.

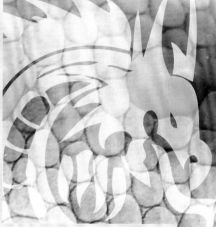

The bearded dragon has spiky scales on its throat.
The bearded dragon inflates his "beard" like a balloon.
This is how he scares his enemies.

The Chinese water dragon loves to swim.

Alligators and Crocodiles

What's the difference?

alligator

crocodile

Alligators have short wide heads in the shape of a U.
Crocodile heads are long and pointed like the letter V.
Both alligators and crocodiles spend most of their time in the water.

The gharial is a crocodile with a long skinny snout.
The gharial has more than one hundred teeth in its mouth.

The saltwater crocodile is the world's biggest reptile!

Baby Reptiles

Sea turtle mothers bury their eggs on the beach.
When the eggs hatch, the baby turtles race to the sea.
A sea turtle may lay one hundred eggs at one time.
That's a lot of brothers and sisters!

Crocodile moms protect their babies.
A crocodile mother carries a baby in her mouth to keep him safe.
Sometimes, the baby rides on her back.

Reptiles **QUIZ**

1. Which is NOT a reptile?
   a) Snake
   b) Frog
   c) Turtle

2. What do chameleons use to catch their food?
   a) Tail
   b) Claws
   c) Tongue

3. How do reptiles keep warm?
   a) By wrapping their bodies in leaves
   b) By resting in a sunny area
   c) By huddling with other reptiles

4. Which snake squeezes its prey?
   a) Boa
   b) Rattlesnake
   c) King cobra

5. Which reptile has special toes that help it climb up walls?
   a) Chameleon
   b) Gecko
   c) Draco lizard

6. What is the world's largest lizard?
   a) Draco lizard
   b) Komodo dragon
   c) Bearded dragon

GLOSSARY

fangs: sharp teeth snakes use to deliver venom

habitat: place where an animal lives

prey: animals that are hunted by other animals for food

scales: thin, flat structures that make up a snake's skin

venom: poison produced by some snakes

viper: a type of snake that has venom

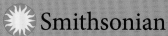
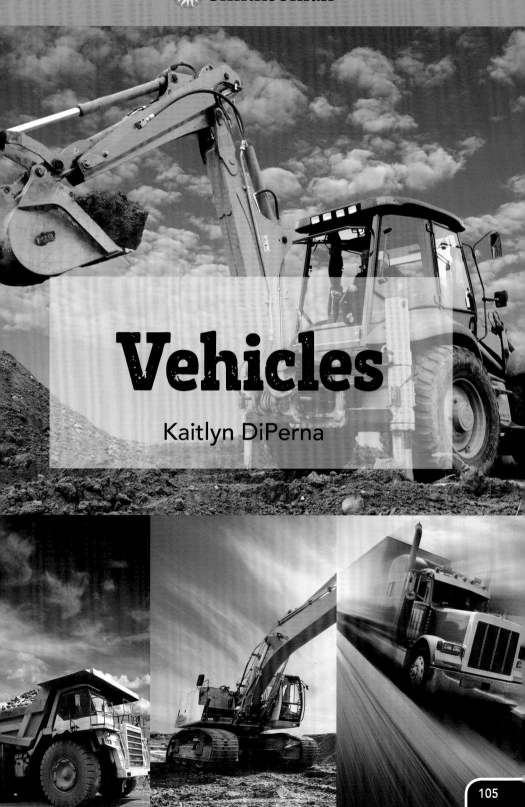

Vehicles

Kaitlyn DiPerna

CONTENTS

Vehicles on the Road

Some vehicles move people or things.

Some vehicles help in emergencies.

And some vehicles help to build roads.

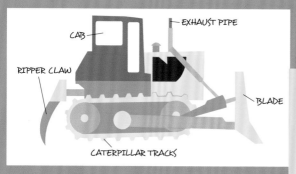

CAB — EXHAUST PIPE

RIPPER CLAW — BLADE

CATERPILLAR TRACKS

Bulldozers use their blades to push dirt or rocks out of the way.

Bulldozers have **caterpillar tracks**. Caterpillar tracks are bands of treads that go around the wheels. The wheels spin the tracks.

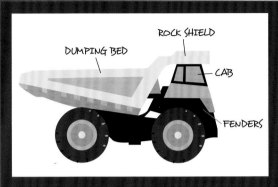

DUMPING BED

ROCK SHIELD

CAB

FENDERS

A dump truck has a box at the back called a bed.
The bed can hold heavy rocks, sand, or dirt.

The bed lifts up. The truck dumps all the rocks, sand, or dirt out!

Dig and Scoop: Backhoe

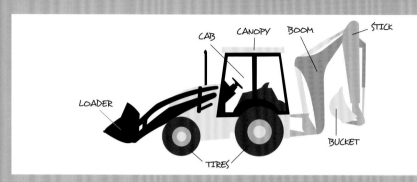

CAB • CANOPY • BOOM • STICK
LOADER • TIRES • BUCKET

A backhoe does two jobs.

In the front is a scoop, called a loader.
The loader can carry dirt, rocks, and gravel.

In the back is a hoe.
The hoe can bend and dig.

Deep Digger: Excavator

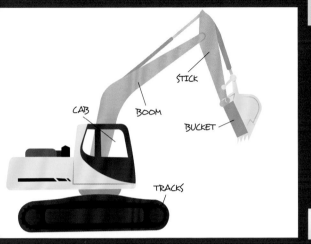

An excavator is like a giant shovel.

The driver sits in the cab.
The cab can spin all the way around.

Smooth It Over: Grader

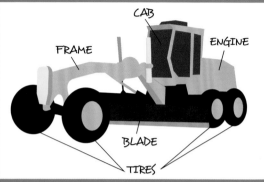

FRAME
CAB
ENGINE
BLADE
TIRES

A grader has a giant blade between the front and back **axles**.

The blade smoothes out the ground to make it flat.
Then a road can be built.

Road Roller: Steamroller

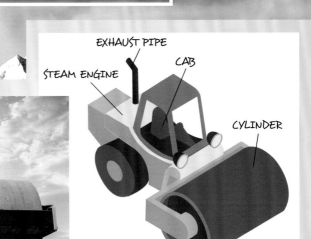

EXHAUST PIPE

STEAM ENGINE

CAB

CYLINDER

A steamroller helps build new roads.

Big, heavy **cylinders** flatten the road.

Some steamrollers have cylinders that can be filled with water.
The water makes the cylinders even heavier!

All Mixed Up: Concrete Mixer

A concrete mixer has a big drum on the back.

Cement dust, rocks, sand, and water are loaded into the drum.
Then the drum spins to mix the ingredients.
The ingredients make concrete!

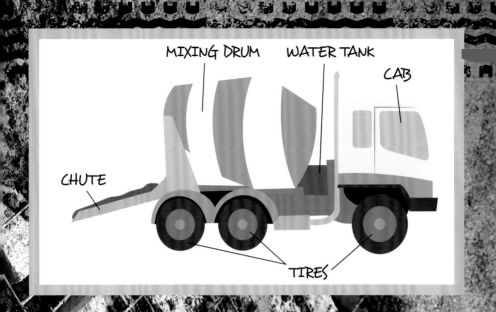

MIXING DRUM   WATER TANK

CAB

CHUTE

TIRES

Wet concrete is poured down the chute.

The concrete is smoothed so it dries flat.

Why Up High: Cherry Picker

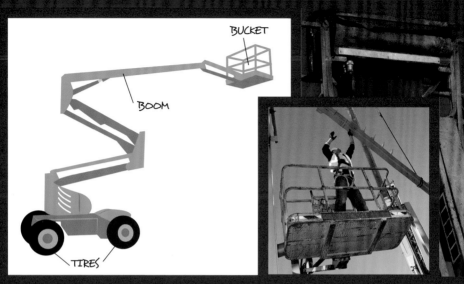

BUCKET

BOOM

TIRES

A cherry picker has a bucket that lifts high into the air.

These machines were used to pick cherries from tall trees.

Today, cherry pickers are used to get to anything up high.

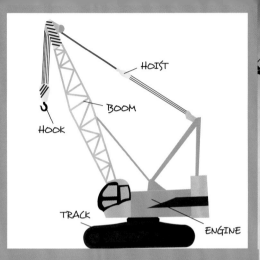

HOIST

BOOM

HOOK

TRACK

ENGINE

A crane lifts loads up, down, and from side to side.

A crane can lift a heavy load to the top of a building.
A crane can move a piano out of a high apartment.

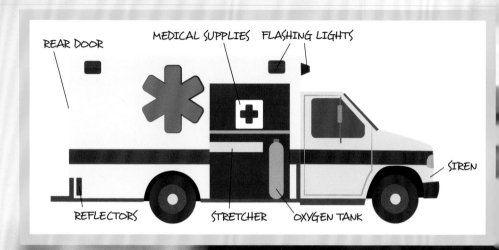

REAR DOOR

MEDICAL SUPPLIES   FLASHING LIGHTS

SIREN

REFLECTORS   STRETCHER   OXYGEN TANK

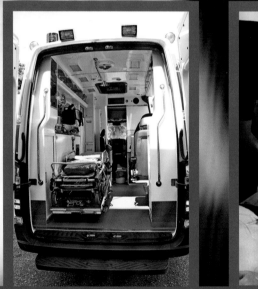

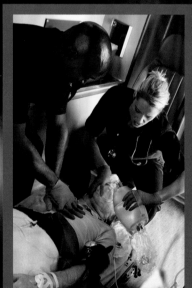

An ambulance has supplies that help people who are hurt.
The ambulance crew helps treat them.

The ambulance crew calls the hospital. "We are on our way!"

An ambulance has flashing lights. An ambulance has loud sirens.

The lights and sirens tell other cars to move over.

Then the ambulance can get to the hospital faster.

Fighting Fires: Fire Engines

Fire engines are used to fight fires. Different kinds of fire engines have different jobs.

A pumper pumps water from a hydrant.

A tanker has a tank full of water.

A ladder truck has a long ladder that can reach tall buildings.

SIREN

LADDER

CAB

FIRE DEPT

FIRE HOSE

Fire engines carry lots of tools.

An axe can chop down doors.

A two-way radio lets fire fighters communicate.

A hydrant wrench turns on hydrants.

The Jaws of Life can cut through metal.

EMERGENCY GEAR

FLASHING LIGHTS

POLICE

Can you guess why some police cars are called panda cars?

Police cars **patrol** the streets to keep them safe.

Police cars have powerful engines so they can get to an emergency quickly.

Police cars have sirens and flashing lights.

Police cars have computers, cameras, and two-way radios.
Police cars carry weapons and tools for emergencies.

Some police cars carry police dogs!

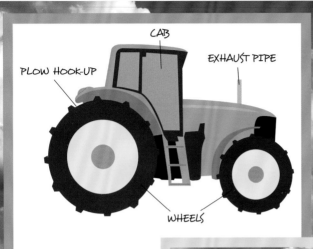

CAB

EXHAUST PIPE

PLOW HOOK-UP

WHEELS

Tractors have big wheels.
Big wheels help a tractor on rough dirt.

Tractors are strong.
They can pull heavy plows.

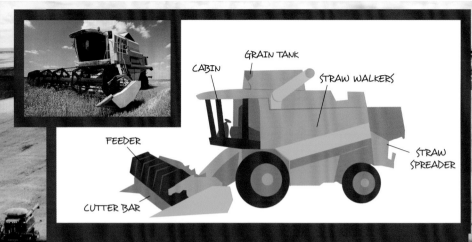

GRAIN TANK

CABIN

STRAW WALKERS

FEEDER

STRAW SPREADER

CUTTER BAR

To **harvest** means to gather **crops**.

A combine harvester combines three farm jobs into one machine.

It cuts the crops.
It gathers the crops.
It separates the crops into parts we eat and parts we don't eat.

Trash Time! Garbage Truck

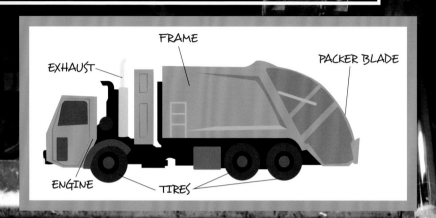

FRAME

EXHAUST

PACKER BLADE

ENGINE

TIRES

RECYCLING

A garbage truck picks up trash from homes.
Then it brings the trash to a dump or recycling center.

Front loader trucks can pick up dumpsters.
A big **compactor** presses the trash down to make more room.

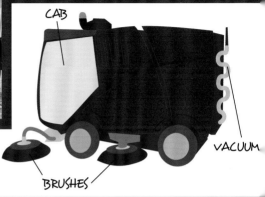

CAB

VACUUM

BRUSHES

A street sweeper cleans the streets.

A street sweeper picks up trash with a vacuum.
Then it cleans the streets with water and brushes.

Big Rig: Eighteen-Wheeler

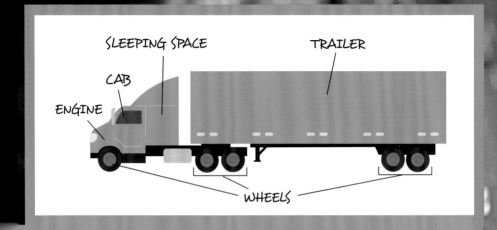

SLEEPING SPACE

TRAILER

CAB

ENGINE

WHEELS

Eighteen-wheelers have lots of names. They can be called tractor-trailers, semitrailers, or big rigs.

Eighteen-wheelers have a cab in the front.
The driver sits in the cab.
Some cabs have a space for sleeping.

Eighteen-wheelers have a trailer in the back.
The trailer holds loads of food, toys, clothes, or whatever is being delivered.

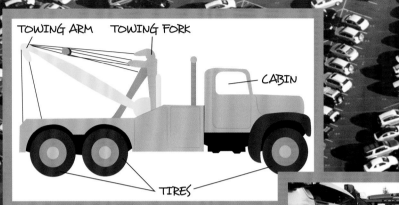

TOWING ARM   TOWING FORK

CABIN

TIRES

A tow truck **transports** a broken-down vehicle.

Some tow trucks pull the vehicle on a hook or sling.

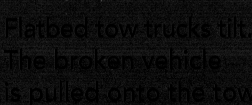

Flatbed tow trucks tilt. The broken vehicle is pulled onto the tow truck's bed.

ADJUSTABLE RAMPS

CAB

TRAILERS

A car carrier can carry up to nine cars or trucks!

Cars have to be driven up the ramps and onto the platforms.
Then the platforms can be raised up and tilted.

Let it Snow! Snowplow

BED FULL OF SAND

LIGHTS

PLOW BLADE

SAND SPREADER

Snowplows have big blades that push snow out of the way.

Snowplows carry sand in their beds. A sand spreader sprays sand on the road. Sand stops cars and trucks from slipping on icy patches.

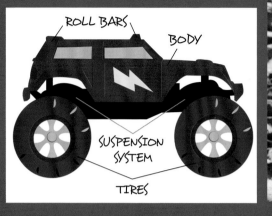

ROLL BARS

BODY

SUSPENSION SYSTEM

TIRES

Monster trucks can be twelve feet high! Monster truck tires are more than five feet tall!

Monster truck shows have events like car-crushing and jumping.

Monster trucks have names like King Kong and Bigfoot!

133

Vehicles QUIZ

1. Which vehicle is used to get to anything up high?
   a) Cherry picker
   b) Bulldozer
   c) Steam roller

2. Which job can a backhoe NOT do?
   a) Flatten roads
   b) Carry dirt, rocks, and gravel
   c) Bend and dig

3. Which vehicle cuts, gathers, and separates crops?
   a) Tractor
   b) Combine harvester
   c) Garbage truck

4. Which vehicle cleans streets?
   a) Street sweeper
   b) Grader
   c) Fire truck

5. What vehicle is also called a "big rig"?
   a) Excavator
   b) Monster truck
   c) Eighteen-wheeler

6. Which vehicle can carry up to nine cars or trucks?
   a) Tow truck
   b) Car carrier
   c) Dump truck

Answers: 1) a 2) a 3) b 4) a 5) c 6) b

GLOSSARY

axles: rods that spin wheels

caterpillar tracks: bands of treads that go around the wheels

compactor: a machine that presses waste down to make it smaller

crops: plants that are grown and harvested

cylinders: shapes with curved surfaces and circle ends

harvest: to gather crops

patrol: to keep watch over an area

transports: brings from one place to another

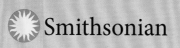
Smithsonian

Safari Animals

Emily Rose Oachs

CONTENTS

African Savanna Life

Savannas are grassy lands.
Savannas have few trees.
Africa has large areas of savanna.

Many animals live on Africa's savannas.

Lions are big cats.
They live in groups called **prides**.

Male lions have long fur on their necks.
This fur is called a **mane**.

Lions make loud sounds.
They can be heard from far away.
"Roar!"

Giraffes: View From Up High

Giraffes are very tall animals.
They have long legs.
They have long necks.

They eat leaves and fruit from tall trees.

Giraffes stretch out their tongues.
Their tongues are long and thin.
Their tongues grab leaves to eat.

Graceful Gazelles

Gazelles are graceful animals.
They run very fast.
They leap across the savanna.

Gazelles have big, sharp horns.
Sometimes gazelles fight each other.
They use their horns to fight.

Flamingos live in huge groups.

Flamingos have pink feathers.
Their food makes their feathers pink.

Flamingos have long, skinny legs. Sometimes flamingos stand on one leg. This is how they rest.

Elephants: Tremendous Trunks

Elephants are the biggest animals on land.

Elephants have two **tusks**.
Tusks are large, curved teeth.
They grow out of an elephant's mouth.

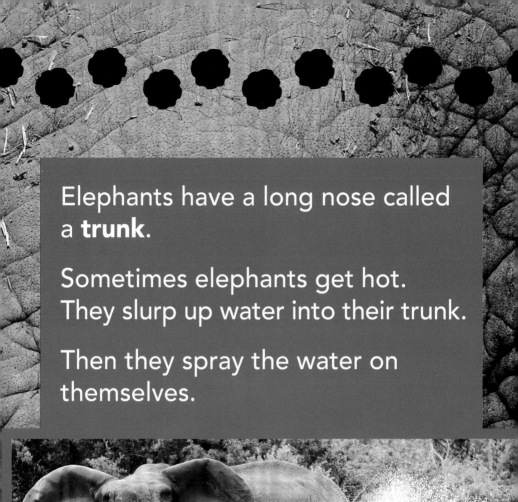

Elephants have a long nose called a **trunk**.

Sometimes elephants get hot. They slurp up water into their trunk.

Then they spray the water on themselves.

Warthogs: Terrifying Tusks

Warthogs are wild pigs.
Warthogs have big noses.

Warthogs sniff for food.
Warthogs eat grass, berries, and roots.

Warthogs have tusks.
The tusks are sharp.
The tusks scare away other animals.

Black Mambas: Fierce Fangs

Black mambas are deadly snakes.
They have long bodies.
They slither quickly across the ground.

Black mambas have sharp fangs.
Black mambas make a poison called
venom.
Black mambas have venom in their
fangs.
Watch out!

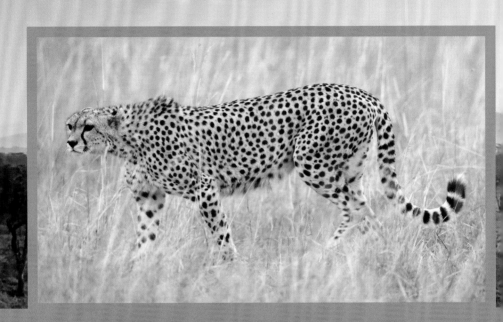

Cheetahs have gold fur and black spots. Their bodies are very strong.

Cheetahs are the fastest animals on land.
They can run as fast as a car!
They sprint to catch prey.
Prey are the animals that cheetahs hunt.

Ostriches: Biggest Birds

Ostriches are the biggest birds in the world.
They are tall and heavy.
They weigh over three hundred pounds!

Ostriches have weak wings.
They cannot fly.

Ostriches have long, strong le
They can run very fast.

Hyenas: Laughter on the Savanna

Hyenas have spotted coats.
Hyenas make odd noises.
It sounds like they are laughing!

Hyenas are **predators**.
Predators hunt other animals for food.
Hyenas hunt gazelles and zebras.

Rhinoceroses are heavy animals.
They have thick gray skin.
They have two horns on their nose.

Rhinoceroses live under the hot sun.
They rest in the shade to cool off.
They also roll in the mud.

Hefty Hippopotamuses

Hippopotamuses have heavy, round bodies.

Hippopotamuses have large mouths.
They open their mouths wide.
This shows off their teeth!

Zebras: Special Stripes

Zebras have black and white stripes. Their manes have stripes too.

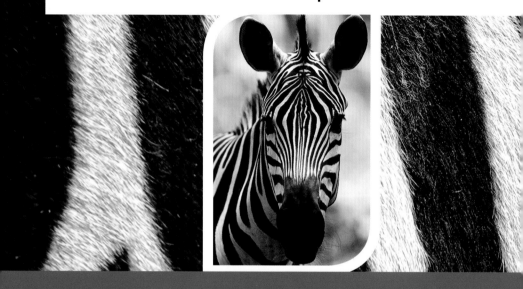

A zebra's stripes are special. No other zebra has the same stripes.

Zebras need to eat a lot.
Their favorite food is grass.
They also eat fruit, roots, and leaves.

Safari Animals QUIZ

1. Which animals live in groups called prides?
   a) Lions
   b) Elephants
   c) Cheetahs

2. What are tusks?
   a) Large curved horns
   b) Large curved teeth
   c) Large curved trunks

3. What is an elephant's long nose called?
   a) Nostril
   b) Snout
   c) Trunk

4. What poison do black mambas make?
   a) Fangs
   b) Venom
   c) Tusks

5. What is the fastest animal on land?
   a) Ostrich
   b) Gazelle
   c) Cheetah

6. Which animal has two horns on its nose?
   a) Warthog
   b) Hippopotamus
   c) Rhinoceros

Answers: 1) a 2) b 3) c 4) b 5) c 6) c

GLOSSARY

mane: long hair that grows on an animal's neck

predators: animals that eat other animals

prides: groups of lions

trunk: a long nose

tusks: long, pointed teeth that grow out of a mouth

venom: a poison that some animals make

Insects

Ruth Strother

CONTENTS

Introduction to Insects

Insects live all around the world.
Some insects help plants grow.
Some insects help make soil.
Some insects are food for other animals.

The Insect Body

All insects crawl on six legs.
All insects have a hard shell.
Most insects have wings and
antennae.
Antennae help insects sense
what is around them.

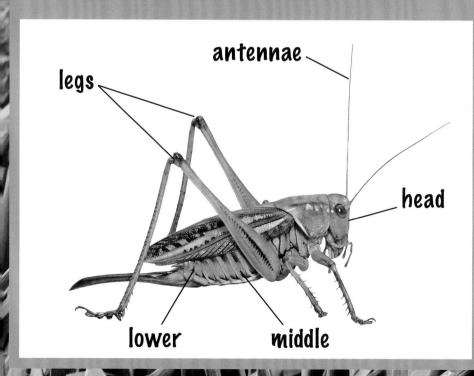

Insects have three main body parts. Insects have a head. Legs and wings grow from their middle part. The lower part is where some insects hear and breathe!

antennae

legs

head

lower

middle

Life Cycle

eggs

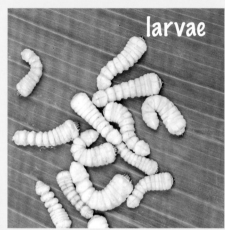

larvae

All insects hatch out of eggs.

Then some insects become **larvae**. Larvae look like worms.

nymph

But some insects become **nymphs** instead. Nymphs look like small adults.

Larvae and nymphs eat a lot.

Then larvae become **pupae**.
Pupae do not move or eat.
Pupae and nymphs grow into adult
insects.

pupae

Insect Homes

bee hive

ant tunnel

Bees and wasps live in hives.
Ants live in tunnels in the ground.

termite hill

And termites live in sandy hills.

Some insects just dig into the soil. Some insects hide on plants.

grasshopper

Many monarch butterflies gather on a tree to rest.

Moths Are Not Butterflies

Most butterflies are full of color.

Most moths are gray or tan.

Butterflies have nubs on the tips of their antennae.

Moths have straight or feathery antennae.

Butterflies are out during the day.

Most moths are active at night.

Butterflies rest with their wings folded up.

Moths rest with their wings spread.

But butterflies and most moths drink **nectar** from flowers.

Bees, Wasps, and Hornets

wasp

stinger

Bees, wasps, and hornets are
stinging insects.
They live in big family groups
called **colonies**.
They protect a queen.
The queen lives deep in the nest.

The nest can be a hive.
Some wasps make their hive from pape
Some make their hive from mud.

Honeybees drink from flowers.
Honeybees turn the flower's nectar
into honey.

Ants, Termites, and Cockroaches

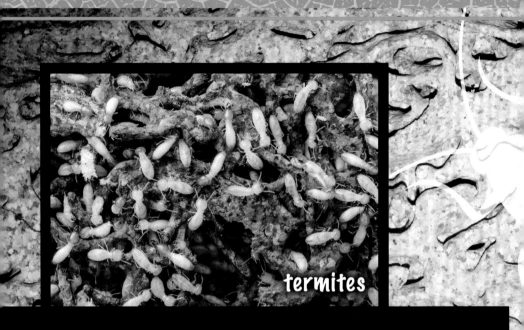
termites

Ants and termites live in colonies too.
The queen lays eggs. The males mate
with the queen.
The females protect and feed the
whole colony.

ants

cockroach

Termites look like ants. But termites are more like cockroaches.
Cockroaches live alone, though.
Ants, termites, and cockroaches like to live in people's homes.

Beetles

Beetles have hard shells.
Beetles have strong jaws too.
Beetles have two sets of wings.
They only use one set of wings to fly.

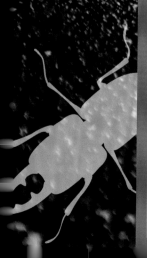

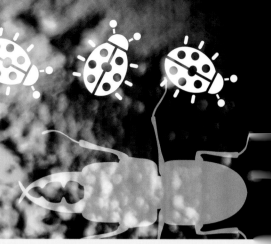

Most beetles use sounds and odors to "talk" to each other.

Fireflies light up.

Ladybugs squirt stinky yellow blood to keep enemies away.

Grasshoppers, Crickets, and Mantises

grasshopper

Grasshoppers and crickets have long back legs.
Long legs help them jump far.
But grasshoppers have shorter antennae then crickets do.

cricket

Praying mantises jump too.
Praying mantises jump to catch other insects to eat.
They use their large front legs to grab the insects.

Flies and Gnats

Flies taste with their feet.
Flies spit saliva onto their food.
Then they suck it up.
Flies spread germs.

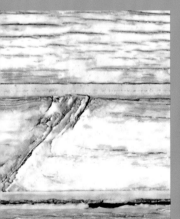

Flies are pests.
Gnats are pests too.
Tiny gnats fly in groups.
They fly into our eyes and ears.
But gnats are not harmful.

Fleas and Mosquitoes

Fleas and mosquitoes need blood to live.

Fleas are tiny insects.

Fleas can jump quickly and far. Fleas poke their mouth into skin to drink blood.

Flea bites itch.

Female mosquitoes suck blood. They suck blood to feed their eggs.

Mosquitos can carry germs that make people sick.

Stick Insects, Dragonflies, and Cicadas

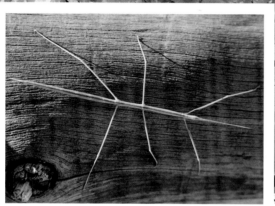

Stick insects are hard to see.
They look like tree twigs.
Sticks are the longest insects alive today.

Dragonflies are great fliers.
They hunt and eat in midair!

Thousands of cicadas gather.
The males make a clicking sound.
They also make a drumming sound.
Cicadas are noisy!

Harmful Insects

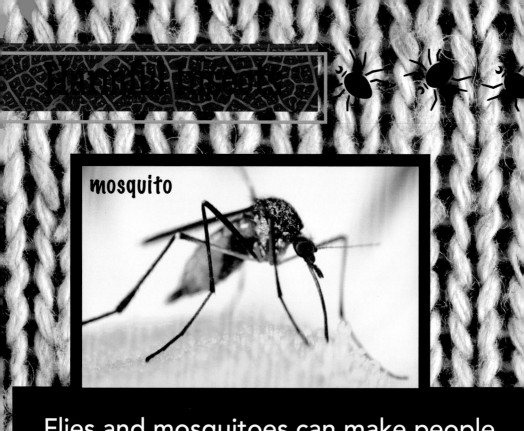

mosquito

Flies and mosquitoes can make people sick.
Bees and wasps can sting.
Some insects can be harmful to people.

wasp

grasshopper eating leaves

Grasshoppers can kill crops. Termites can damage homes. Moths can eat through clothes. Some insects can be harmful to people's property.

termites eating wood

Helpful Insects

Honeybees make tasty honey.
Honeybees also help flowers grow.

Ants make our soil better.
And silkworms make silk.

Dragonflies eat mosquitoes.
Ladybugs eat aphids.
Aphids kill plants in our gardens.

Some insects can be helpful to us.
Some people even eat insects!

Insects QUIZ

1. How many legs do insects have?
   a) Six
   b) Four
   c) Eight

2. What helps insects sense what is around them?
   a) Antennae
   b) Larvae
   c) Tongue

3. What insect doesn't live in a colony?
   a) Bees
   b) Ants
   c) Cockroach

4. Which insect drinks blood?
   a) Praying mantis
   b) Mosquito
   c) Grasshopper

5. Which insect hunts and eats in midair?
   a) Wasp
   b) Ant
   c) Dragonfly

6. What insect can be harmful to people?
   a) Mosquito
   b) Butterfly
   c) Ladybug

Answers: 1) a 2) a 3) c 4) b 5) c 6) a

GLOSSARY

antennae: a pair of organs on an insect's head used for sensing objects around them

colonies: groups of animals or insects living together

larvae: insects in their young, wormlike form

nectar: the sweet fluid some insects drink from flowers

nymphs: young insects that look like small adults

pupae: insects in the stage where they change from larvae to adults

LEVEL GUIDELINES

LEVEL 1: EARLY READERS

- Basic factual texts with familiar themes and content
- Concepts in text are reinforced by photos
- Includes glossary to reinforce reading comprehension
- Phonic regularity
- Simple sentence structure and repeated sentence patterns
- Easy vocabulary familiar to kindergarteners and first-graders

LEVEL 2: DEVELOPING READERS

- Simple factual texts with mostly familiar themes and content
- Concepts in text are supported by images
- Includes glossary to reinforce reading comprehension
- Repetition of basic sentence structure with variation of placement of subjects, verbs, and adjectives
- Introduction to new phonic structures
- Integration of contractions, possessives, compound sentences, and some three-syllable words
- Mostly easy vocabulary familiar to kindergarteners and first-graders